PLATFORM PAPERS

QUARTERLY ESSAYS ON THE PERFORMING ARTS FROM CURRENCY HOUSE

||||||||||||||||||||||||||||||||||||||||||||||||||||||||||||||||||||

No. 52
August 2017

CURRENCY HOUSE

Platform Papers Partners

Platform Papers
Readers' Forum

Readers' responses to our previous essays are posted on our website. Contributions to the conversation (250 to 2000 words) may be emailed to info@currencyhouse. org.au. The Editor welcomes opinion and criticism in the interest of healthy debate but reserves the right to monitor where necessary.

Platform Papers, quarterly essays on the performing arts, is published every February, May, August and November and is available through bookshops, by subscription and on line in paper or electronic version. For details see our website at www.currencyhouse.org.au.

PUTTING WORDS IN THEIR MOUTHS:
The playwright and screenwriter at work

ANDREW BOVELL

ABOUT THE AUTHOR

Andrew Bovell's career over thirty years has won him many awards and taken him around the world. His latest work for the stage, *Things I Know to be True* premiered in Adelaide in May 2016 in a co-production between The State Theatre Company and UK-based, Frantic Assembly. The production opened in London at the Lyric Hammersmith in September before touring the UK. It returns to the Lyric and an extensive UK tour later in 2017.

His widely acclaimed adaptation of Kate Grenville's novel *The Secret River* premiered at the Roslyn Packer Theatre at the 2013 Sydney Festival. The Sydney Theatre Company production was directed by Neil Armfield. It toured to the Centenary of Canberra Festival and Perth International Arts Festival, won six Helpmann Awards including Best Play, as well as Best New Work, at the Sydney Theatre Awards; an Awgie Award for Stage Writing; the David Williamson Prize; and it was joint winner of the NSW Premier's Literary Award for Community Relations. It returned to the Roslyn Packer Theatre in 2016 before touring to Brisbane and Melbourne. It was revived again for the 2017 Adelaide Festival of the Arts where it was performed in the Anstey Quarry.

When the Rain Stops Falling premiered at the 2008

Adelaide Festival of the Arts, produced by Brink Productions, before touring nationally. The play has been produced in London at the Almeida Theatre (2009) and in New York at the Lincoln Centre (2010) where it won five Lucille Lortell Awards and was named best new play of the year by *Time Magazine*. His play *Speaking in Tongues* (1996) won an AWGIE and was internationally successful before being adapted into his groundbreaking movie *Lantana* (2001). Earlier works for the stage include *Holy Day, Who's Afraid of the Working Class, Scenes From a Separation, Shades of Blue, Ship of Fools, After Dinner, The Ballad of Lois Ryan* and *State of Defence*. The Sydney Theatre Company revived his early play, *After Dinner*, for a sell-out season at the Wharf Theatre in Sydney in 2015.

His most recent film is the French language *In the Shadow of Iris,* directed by Jalil Lespert (2017). *A Most Wanted Man* is an adaptation of the John Le Carré novel directed by Anton Corbijn and starring Philip Seymour Hoffman. The film premiered at the 2014 Sundance Film Festival. Other films include *Edge of Darkness, Blessed, The Book of Revelation, Head On, Lust, The Fisherman's Wake, Piccolo Mondo, Strictly Ballroom* and the multi-award winning *Lantana*.

In 2017 Andrew Bovell was awarded the Patrick White Fellowship for an established playwright by the Sydney Theatre Company.

Acknowledgments

The Mouths that Spoke the Words

I would like to acknowledge all the actors who have spoken my words, even those who on occasion forgot them. The first actor to perform a role in a new play has a particularly important task and I owe an enormous debt to them. Some of those actors are acknowledged below.

Martin in *State of Defence* was played by Michael White. The play was first performed in the lunch room at the Jolimont train maintenance yard in 1987.

Bob Pavlich played the Fool in *Ship of Fools*. The play was directed by Robert Draffin and premiered at the 1988 Adelaide Festival Fringe before returning to Melbourne for a season at Anthill Theatre. The play was revived in a new production, directed by Ros Horin in 1999 for Griffin Theatre Company.

Leigh Morgan played Monika in the original production of *After Dinner*. The play was directed by Kim Durban and premiered at La Mama, Carlton in 1988. Helen Thomson played the role in the 2015 Sydney Theatre Company production, directed by Imara Savage.

The original cast members of *Speaking in Tongues* were Elaine Hudson, Marshall Napier, Glenda Linscott and

Geoff Morrell. The play was directed by Ros Horin for the Griffin Theatre and premiered at the Stables Theatre, Sydney, in 1996.

Rhonda in *Who's Afraid of the Working Class?* was played by Eugenia Fragos. The play was directed by Julian Meyrick and premiered at the Victorian Trades Hall in Carlton in May 1998.

Anthony La Paglia played Leon Zat in *Lantana*. The film was directed by Ray Lawrence and produced by Jan Chapman. It premiered on the opening night of the Sydney Film Festival in June 2001

Nora Ryan was played by Kerry Walker in the original production of *Holy Day*. It was directed by Rosabla Clemente for the State Theatre Company of South Australia and premiered at the Dunstan Playhouse in 2001. In 2003, Pamela Rabe played the role in the Sydney Theatre Company production, directed by Ariette Taylor. Obedience in *Holy Day* was played by Melody Reynolds in 2001 and by Natasha Wanganeen in 2003.

Neil Pigot played Gabriel York in the original production of *When the Rain Stops Falling*. The play was directed by Chris Drummond for Brink Productions and premiered at the 2008 Adelaide Festival of the Arts.

Ursula Yovich played Dhirrumbin in the original production of *The Secret River*. The play was directed by Neil Armfield for the Sydney Theatre Company and premiered at the Roslyn Packer Theatre for the 2013 Sydney Festival. Ningali Lawford-Wolf played the role in the 2016 remount in Sydney and subsequent tour to Melbourne and Brisbane. She returned to the role for the

2017 Adelaide Festival of the Arts.

Bob Price was first played by Paul Blackwell in the State Theatre Company of SA and Frantic Assembly production of *Things I Know to be True*. The play was co-directed by Geordie Brookman and Scott Graham and premiered at the Dunstan Playhouse in May 2016. Bob was later played by Ewan Stewart in the English version of the same production, which opened in September 2016 at the Lyric Hammersmith. Mark Price was played by Tim Walter in the 2016 Adelaide season and by Matthew Barker in the UK tour. Fran Price was played by Eugenia Fragos in the Adelaide production and by Imogen Stubbs in the English production. Pip Price was played by Georgia Adamson in the Adelaide production and by Natalie Casey in the English production.

1. Introduction

I put words in their mouths. It is this, more than anything else that distinguishes what I do as a playwright and screenwriter from the work of the novelist, or the poet, or the short story writer. They write their words primarily to be read. I write mine primarily, to be said and heard. I rely on the work of the actor, the vision of the director and designers and the presence of the audience. Without them, my work remains as just words on a page. Nevertheless, I work to ensure that every one of those words counts.

> *I do not believe in God. I do not believe in miracles. I cannot explain this.*
>
> Gabriel York, *When the Rain Stops Falling* (2008)

These are the first words spoken in the play *When the Rain Stops Falling*. We are in the town of Alice Springs in the year 2039. A bewildered Gabriel York stands holding a large fish, which has just fallen from the sky and landed at his feet. We will soon learn that in 2039 fish are close to extinction. Certainly, they no longer appear on the tables of the common people. What fish do remain in the sea are reserved for the tables of the extremely wealthy. The question is whether this fish, which has fallen from the sky in the middle of the Australian desert, is a portent of the end of the world or tomorrow's lunch?

It is said of some writers that their characters are simply different versions of themselves. I don't know whether that's true in my case. There are certainly some characters with whom I feel an affinity. They are usually the ones asking the questions: How did I get here? What just happened? What am I meant to do now? Gabriel York is one such character. Life has bewildered him and yet he shows great courage in trying to make sense of it.

As I sit here and look back at all that I have written and forward to what I am still to write, Gabriel's words could be my own in describing my career as a writer: 'I do not believe in God. I do not believe in miracles. I cannot explain this.'

In becoming a writer, a metaphorical fish fell at my feet. I am still surprised. Still bewildered. I don't know where it came from. I don't particularly know what it means. I just know that it is a fish.

This Platform Paper is an attempt to explain the nature of that fish. It will be in part a history, in part a manifesto and in part a love letter to those who have made what I do possible.

2. Early Landscapes

Look at it! Endless fucking plain.
Soon a thousand flowers will bloom.
It's a bastard to trick us like that. To
make us forget what easy death lies
out there.

Nora, *Holy Day* (2001)

My childhood and adolescence were dominated by two contrasting landscapes, the endless plains of the Western Australian wheatbelt and the coastal suburbs of Perth with the Indian Ocean at the end of my street. The tension between the interior of our continent and our vast coastline sits at the heart of the Australian psyche and has provided both a thematic and a literal terrain for many Australian writers to explore. I count myself among them and both landscapes have influenced the writer I have become.

I was born in Kalgoorlie and my childhood was spent in the small towns on what was known as the wheatbelt. This was marginal land bordering on desert. It had been cleared long ago to grow wheat, barley and sheep. There were good years and bad years and the summers were long and hot. My parents worked for the Bank of New South Wales, later to become Westpac. My father, Peter, eventually became a bank manager, and my mother, Maureen, had stopped work as a teller at eighteen upon marrying my father, as women were then required to do. Ten years later she was raising four children. I was the youngest and the only boy.

Every eighteen months to two years the bank transferred my father to a different town. My mother was always packing up one bank house and moving into a new one. My sisters, Sally, Penny and Jane, were always being settled into new schools and making new friends.

These towns were about as far from anywhere else as you could possibly be. Life on the farms, in particular was incredibly isolated. The people were stoic, resilient and self-reliant. It was the quintessential Western Australian country life. Reg Cribb, a fellow West Australian playwright, had a similar upbringing. Like me his father was a Bank of New South Wales manager and they moved from town to town. Once, we discussed why such a life would produce a couple of playwrights. We agreed that there was a lot of space and time out there and that perhaps we had learned to fill both with vivid imaginations.

My parents both left school at 14. They lived in a time when you could do so and still expect a secure white-collar career path, at least if you were a man. They were not learned people in an academic sense. A tertiary education was neither expected nor was it even aspired to. Whilst their interests grew over the course of their lives and they became avid readers, they were not intellectuals. The point is neither am I. That is not the culture from which I come. I make this point for it is often assumed that our writers and our literary figures come from learned backgrounds. Many do, of course. But not me. I speak from a different place. Nor can I claim an authentic or romanticised working-class heritage as a foundation to some oppositional voice to the establishment. And there is no convict history with which I can adorn my personal narrative. If you push back through the generations of my family you will find shopkeepers, clerks, policemen and nurses all the way. I am from the middle. White. Protestant. Suburban. There is seemingly nothing exceptional here to draw on as a writer. And yet, like fellow Western Australian writers with similar backgrounds, Tim Winton, Robert Drewe, Dorothy Hewett, Reg Cribb and Kate Mulvany, it is the capacity to find the story within the seemingly unexceptional that distinguishes our work.

> *It wasn't meant to be like this… I thought*
> *they'd be like us. But better than us. Better*
> *versions of us. Better educated. With better*
> *jobs. And better prospects. That's what we*
> *worked so hard for. Wasn't it? But I thought*
> *they'd all live close by. In the same city at*
> *least. In a house they built. Just like us. And*
> *that they'd get married to good people. And*
> *have kids. Like us. And that we'd put on a*
> *barbecue here most Sundays. And there*
> *would be all the kids. All the cousins. And that*
> *there'd be cricket. And totem tennis. And sleep-*
> *overs at Nan and Pop's. You know. And*
> *engagements. And weddings. Here in this garden.*
> *That I made. I thought that's what life would be.*
> *That's all I wanted it to be, Fran.*
>
> Bob Price, *Things I Know to be True* (2016)

Eventually my mother became tired of packing and unpacking boxes. I think, too, that she had become tired of being the bank manager's wife. She wanted more and she wasn't going to find it in a country town. It was the 1970s and the role of women was changing and I think she wanted to be a part of it. And so we moved to Grant Street, in North Cottesloe, a hop, skip and a jump from the Indian Ocean. Cottesloe is now one of Perth's salubrious suburbs with its ocean views and lifestyle. But we lived at the wrong end of the suburb and North Cott was tougher terrain then.

Growing up in the suburbs of Perth was violent and tribal. Which tribe you belonged to depended on where you lived, what school you went to and what sport you played. Violence was ritualised on the football field and became a free-for-all at the alcohol and dope-fuelled parties on the weekend. If you wanted to surf you had to fight for your waves. And if you took someone's wave it was sorted out at the pub that night with a pool cue over your head. And if you looked at the wrong girl, 'then you had the shit beaten out of you'. By year nine, aged 14, I was stealing my father's cigarettes from his pack, his change from his bedside table, his beer from the fridge and his car from the carport as soon as he fell asleep. And I was one of the good boys. This is not an unusual adolescence for an Australian boy. The suburbs didn't offer many options and you needed to be strong to break free of the orthodoxies that defined masculinity at the time.

There was another kind of tribe, the kids that did art and drama. They were the smart kids. They were in the top classes at school. They studied languages and musical instruments and English Literature. They grew up in houses with books on the shelves. You would think, given what and who I have become, that I would have sought entry to that tribe. But I simply never considered it. I didn't know I had that choice. But nor, I imagine, did they consider me as being somebody whom they could invite into their tribe. I don't know whether it was the exclusion from such clubs that drove my anti-intellectualism, and to a degree still does; or whether it was my anti-intellectualism that caused me to look elsewhere for enlightenment.

I was looking for something. That's for sure. My mother was smart enough to know it. She also knew that I was going off the rails and needed 'taking in hand'. And so she sent me back to what she knew—the country.

Each summer, for the rest of my high-school years, I was sent to a wheat and sheep farm, outside of the town of Narembeen, 300 ks east of Perth. It was my mother's intention to keep me out of trouble over the long holidays. It worked most of the time. The farm belonged to family friends, Bet and Brian Price. They were good people who worked hard and enjoyed a laugh. Their children, Barry and Toot were older than me and I looked up to them both. I came from a house full of sisters and Barry slotted into the role of big brother without complaint. On the farm I rode the harvester, learned how to shift a bag of wheat, fire a gun, fix a fence, ride a motorbike, round up sheep, catch gilgies (yabbies), slaughter a sheep and butcher it into a month's supply of meat. But more importantly, I learned how to be on my own, an essential lesson for a writer. I learned about the nature of solitude.

Something about those flat endless fields of wheat, the ruins of a settler's crude shack in a back paddock, the golden sunsets, the silence of the bush on a hot day, and the stillness of a dusty shearing shed, brought out something soulful and romantic in me. Maybe it was just a natural part of growing up but out there, in the emptiness I began to think more deeply about things. It's a long time since I've been back to Narembeen but the landscape and the people have stayed with me.

> *With dawn light at the window*
> *Look… Is there any place where the*
> *dawn is more beautiful than this?*
> *When I see the light hit this earth,*
> *Mrs Wilkes, I want to cry… I do. An*
> *old bitch like me wants to cry.*
>
> Nora, *Holy Day* (2001)

One final adolescent landscape contributed to my developing sensibility as a writer. At seventeen, I went to South Africa as an exchange student and lived in a goldmining town east of Johannesburg, called Springs. It was 1980, the dying days of the apartheid regime. The Soweto riots had taken place only four years before. Nelson Mandela was still in prison. Steve Biko's murder was still being denied, and there was growing racial tension in Kwa Thema, the township near where I lived. White South Africans were deeply divided, not only between Afrikaners and English but between those who knew change had to happen and those prepared to fight to maintain the regime. The government and its security forces were becoming increasingly repressive and the overwhelming climate was one of tension, fear and paranoia.

Even though I grew up in Western Australia, I had been largely sheltered from our own racial injustices. I had been taught to look away. There was no hiding it in South Africa. I was shocked that such inequality could be based solely on colour and enshrined in law. I was shocked by the 'Whites Only' signs in parks, on transport and on public buildings. I was shocked that Losthia, the Xhosa woman who worked as a domestic in one of the houses I stayed in, had only three days off at Christmas: one day to travel back to her homeland, one day to spend with her children and one day to return to her employment. That was the only time she saw her children all year.

By the time I returned to Australia I had changed. I had been politicised. I enrolled at the University of Western Australia and began a Bachelor of Arts. I began to read, out of choice, for the first time in my life and I started to ask questions about our own history of racial injustice and inequality.

3. Race and History

Understanding our history and its legacy has become a major theme in my work. I have addressed it in three plays, *Holy Day* in 2001, *The Chair* in 2002, which was a part of a larger work called *Fever* co-written with Patricia Cornelius, Melissa Reeves, Irine Vela and Christos Tsiolkas; and *The Secret River*, 2013, a play based on the novel by Kate Grenville.

> *Thornhill saw the old man and raised his gun.*
> *It went off with a puff of smoke. He thought he*
> *must have missed for the old man was still*
> *standing there, with a question on his face.*
> *Thornhill thought to answer, if he knew the*
> *meaning of the question being asked, before the*
> *old man's legs collapsed beneath him and he sat*
> *politely down in the dust. Blood came from his*
> *mouth, just a trickle, like spit but so red. And then*
> *he lay down and kissed the earth with the blood*
> *from his mouth. And a great shocked silence hung*
> *over the lagoon.*
>
> Dhirrumbin, *The Secret River* (2013)

Holy Day, was a more brutal and unforgiving telling of this history. Like *The Secret River,* it culminated in a massacre of indigenous people. But it was as much about the brutalisation of women by men in our history, and the misunderstanding of the landscape by the white colonisers, as it was about race. It took me more than ten years to write. I kept putting it aside—it was too hard and I was too unsure of myself as a writer. I began it in the year of the Bicentenary, 1988, and it had its first production in 2001. *The Secret River* took much less time. I had the book, of course, and I was more confident by then and had greater control of my craft.

Some argued that *The Secret River* was more forgiving of its white protagonists than *Holy Day* was of its characters. Subsequently, its white audience found it easier to identify with these characters than they did with the harsher portraits of 'whiteness' in *Holy Day.* I think this was the point. It was too easy for the audience to dismiss characters such as Goundry in *Holy Day* as monsters and therefore to conclude that the crimes of our history were carried out by 'evil' men. In the Thornhills of *The Secret River,* the white audience encounters a family with whom they can more readily identify. The Thornhills have escaped the brutality and poverty of the English class system and now aspire to a brighter future for their children. But once the audience empathises with the everyman, William Thornhill, given what he does *at the end* of the story, they must then consider whether, if they found themselves in similar circumstances, they too would choose to participate in a massacre, in order to secure that better future. This is a confronting moment in the theatre. We see a connection between then and now; the distance between our forebears and ourselves no longer seems so vast. The play transcends its historical setting and feels uneasily current in its depiction of the relationship between black and white.

Most white people did not participate directly in the massacres of the first Australians, but they were complicit by remaining silent and prospering from the violent dispossession that took place. That complicity and silence has characterised our history and the argument around the extent of it continues to rage.

The interesting question for me as a playwright who has sought to tell this story is which approach is more effective? *Holy Day* is unambiguous in its conclusions and was a powerful story to witness, but *The Secret River* reached a much broader audience and had a more significant cultural impact. Looking at it now, though, I know that I couldn't have written *The Secret River* without having written *Holy Day* first. And the earlier play, dark as it is, is a more poetic writing of our history.

> *It was dusk. The women had come in from gathering and had lit the fires. The children had been with them. They stayed down at the river to play in the last of the light. A group of older men were sitting near a large rock, talking about the activities of the day and about what would be done tomorrow. They would move on from this place soon and join a larger group for ceremony. Some of the younger men had gathered around the fires to see what the women had brought in. They*

were hungry and looking forward to the meal. One grandmother was angry and telling them to wait. Someone looked up and pointed. A white man was coming down the hill toward them. The women started calling the children. Two older girls ran to the river to bring them back. The old men got up and moved to meet the white man. They understood that he was afraid and was trying to warn them. They heard the shots coming from the other way. They looked to see a group of eight white men on horses crossing the river. The two girls that had gone for the children were the first to be shot. Several younger children fell quickly after. The women ran toward their children and were shot in turn. The men ran for their weapons and were cut down. One woman grabbed a small child and managed to hide her in the bush. But when she went back for another she too was shot. When the full brunt of the shooting was over twenty two people lay dead. Twelve of them were children. Another fourteen were injured. Eight had man-aged to escape in the bush. The old woman had been spared. Too old to run and too old to shoot. She sat by the fire and wept. The white men got down from their horses and shot the wounded. They made a pile of the bodies and set it alight. There was one white death. The man who had come to warn them. This is our history.

Obedience, *Holy Day* (2001)

Obedience is a young Indigenous woman who has been taken from her family and country and raised by Nora, owner of the Travellers Rest, as both a daughter and servant. In this scene Obedience becomes the witness to a massacre. At the end of the play, Goundry, the primary antagonist of the play, rapes her and then cuts out her tongue, ensuring her silence. As a theatrical gesture it is as symbolic as it is literal. In *The Secret River*, Dulla Djin, a Dhurag woman also witnesses a massacre. The event is narrated by Dhirrumbin.

> *Someone else survived that day. The one Blackwood called his wife, Dulla Djin. At the sound of the first shot she took her child and sheltered in the bushes where she watched the slaughter unfold. She wanted to turn away. She wanted to run. But she made herself watch. She knew that someone had to see this.*
>
> Dhirrumbin, *The Secret River* (2013)

Here there is a significant change between the two plays. Both women are cast as witnesses to this history. Where Obedience is annihilated and silenced, Dulla Djin escapes the massacre and understands the need to witness it. Importantly too, Dulla Djin escapes with her child, acknowledging the survival and continuity of the indigenous presence and culture. The emphasis here is placed on survival rather than annihilation.

The only fight I ever had with my father was over the question of racism. I declared at the dinner table that Australia was a racist nation. My father disagreed. He held the paternalistic view that we, the white people, were a superior race and needed to look after the Indigenous people because they couldn't look after themselves. Not any more—after all they had suffered. He wasn't without compassion. He understood that what had taken place in the past had been wrong. Perhaps he saw it as an unfortunate consequence of building a nation. It was a commonly held view at the time, and still is. The argument became heated. I pushed him. He stepped back and fell over a chair. I was shocked—probably not as much as he—but all the same I was shocked at my own violence. I was also ashamed because my father was a gentleman and a gentle man. But what was more shameful was that I walked out and left him floundering on the floor. Later, he quietly said: 'You need to watch that temper of yours, son.'

4. Melbourne

At the gate I tell Dad that I will come home soon to visit. And he tells me that he'll come to see me in Sydney as soon as I have settled in. Both of us know that neither of these things will happen but pretending they will seems to make the parting easier. I linger in his embrace knowing that it will be the last time I will be held by him, as a man and then he does something that takes my breath away. He kisses me on the lips. And it almost does me in. It is so intimate. And I have never loved him more.

And I look back from the gate and he has broken. He is weeping. Rosie is holding him. She has him. I have to look away. I have to look ahead. I have to keep walking. My father's grief is a price I am prepared to pay.

The plane turns down the runway, increases its speed, lifts off the ground and as it makes its ascent I look down upon the city where I grew up, and steel myself against memories, against history and against the man I was. By the time I land in Sydney, Mark Price will just be someone I used to know.

Mark Price, *Things I Know to Be True* (2016)

I left Perth in 1984 and like Mark, I knew I wouldn't return to live in the city I was raised in. My transformation was not as profound as Mark's was to be, but it was significant, nonetheless. In Melbourne, I became a playwright.

I was to study at the Victorian College of the Arts. I had been accepted into the short-lived three year Diploma, specialising in playwriting at the School of Drama. It was the only undergraduate training for playwrights in the country and there was a degree of debate around whether training a playwright was possible.

I had never written a play until I wrote one for my application. It was a comedy of manners, based on my own family, an evisceration of my parents' marriage. Unforgivable, really, but I was clearly a natural playwright because nothing was sacred. To my astonishment, I was accepted into the course. I think the play demonstrated a degree of emotional honesty, a good ear for dialogue and an understanding of the rhythms of spoken language. It was something to build on. And I think these three qualities have remained key strengths in my work.

When I read the work of a new writer I look for an understanding of the rhythms of spoken language. For me, *how* something is said is as important as *what* is said. A character that struggles to say something is more interesting to me than a character that speaks with ease and confidence. My characters often speak as if they are unsure of what they are trying to say. It is as if they are discovering what needs to be said while they are saying it. It's the dance of language. Good playwrights understand this and each has their own dance and song that they sing. Harold Pinter has it. Caryl Churchill has it. Arthur Miller and Sarah Kane have it. David Mamet has it. Tennessee Williams has it. Patricia Cornelius has it. Each is particular to them. It is their voice.

Melbourne was a revelation. I was struck by the presence of its history in its streetscapes and the diversity of people in its inner suburbs. It seemed sophisticated and decadent, and intellectual compared to Perth. I found a room, or rather a cupboard, in a terrace house in McArthur Place in Carlton. Jane Turner, the comedienne and actor, lived in the front room and through her I began to discover the thriving Melbourne comedy scene at Le Joke and the Last Laugh. La Mama was just around the corner. I didn't then know the history I had just missed. The Australian Performing Group and the Pram Factory had only just come to their end.

I arrived at the Victorian College of the Arts (VCA) with a fairly traditional understanding of what a playwright did. I imagined that he or she worked in much the same way as a novelist or a poet might. I was about to have that notion turned on its head.

Peter Oyston was no longer the director of the School of Drama. However, his legacy remained. His vision described a training of 'theatre makers', rather than the more traditional understanding of actors, directors and writers. In some ways the course was a reaction to the more established school in Sydney. At the National Institute of Dramatic Art (NIDA), students were trained to supply the existing hierarchical company structures. At VCA the students were trained to go out into the community and to change those structures or make new ones. It was a democratic, egalitarian and collaboratively based approach to making theatre. It was also radical and innately political. To this end, the authorial vision of the playwright was subsumed by the collective vision of the group and the community for which the work was being made. A series of instrumental companies emerged from the school, in the late 1970s and early 1980s such as West, Theatre Works and the Murray River Performing Group.

By 1984 the culture of the school was in transition, under the directorship of Roger Hodgman, who would go on to become artistic director of the Melbourne Theatre Company (MTC). Roger was an early champion of my work. He introduced me to my first agent, Hilary Linstead, and later offered me a position as writer-in-residence at the MTC and in the early 1990s commissioned me to adapt *Gulliver's Travels* for a co-production with Handspan Puppet Theatre. Later, he commissioned Hannie Rayson and me to co-write *Scenes From A Separation,* which was directed by Robyn Nevin at the MTC in 1995 and again in a new production at the Sydney Theatre Company in 2004.

To a degree, having established a playwrights' course, the school was unsure what to do with us (there were only three of us). Fortunately, we were required to do the general theatre course for the first year. And so I shared classes with actors, directors, technicians and designers and, importantly, animateurs—the midwives of the new theatre. The boundaries between these disciplines were, in theory, being challenged and broken down. I was by no means an actor but working alongside them gave me an insight into their process and a sense of being a part of an ensemble of 'theatre practitioners'. The fact that I learned from the beginning how to work with actors and other theatre makers, was a crucial factor in determining the kind of playwright I became.

At VCA I came into contact with some inspirational teachers. Hilary Glow, in her Critical Studies course, taught me about cultural context. The movement teacher, Anne Thompson, revealed how the language of choreography was as important to the writer as it was for the actor and dancer. Nancy Black directed my first full-length work at the college, *An Ordinary Dream about a Journey North.* In this play lay the seeds of the multi-time structure and superimposition used twenty years later in *When the Rain Stops Falling.* The ideas and techniques I was experimenting with at college became the ideas that continued to preoccupy me as a professional playwright.

The performance artist Lyndal Jones was an extraordinary teacher. She brought a cross-disciplinary approach to the idea of making work that encouraged us to look to the visual arts, to dance, to music, to philosophy and to intellectual discourse itself as source material. She introduced us to artists such as Laurie Anderson, whose performance and image-based narratives became significant in my imagination. But it was Richard Murphet's improvisation class that taught me the most about writing. To my surprise, I was good at it. It was all about being in the moment and being open to what comes next. Where many of the acting students gravitated toward the comic, I would push into darker and more emotional terrain. I would raise the stakes in a scene by pulling out a metaphorical gun. And I knew how to build on what was given to me, on the floor. These are the same instincts that serve good writing.

When I write a line of dialogue I don't know always know what the next line will be. Some lines, of course, I know ahead and I need to build to them. But most of the time I don't know what's going to happen next. It is all an improvisation in my head within a broad structure determined by time and place. Later, I learned that this was how Harold Pinter wrote. He began a play with the first line, which then suggested the second and so on until he reached the end of the play. It wasn't until then that he really knew who and what the play was about. I do a little more planning than that but when writing takes you somewhere you weren't expecting to go, it's usually a sign that something is working.

I use the analogy of sculpting. You begin with a lump of wood. Your intention is to carve a house; but as you work, you discover that the grain has certain qualities, that it flows this way rather than that way. And there are other surprises, like a knot in the wood you didn't expect. You can ignore the direction of the grain and you can ignore the knot and keep on carving the house. Or you can follow the grain and use the knot and discover that you're carving a boat instead. By being open to what's possible, writing becomes a process of discovery.

ELIZABETH: *How's the soup?*
GABRIEL: *Fine.*
ELIZABETH: *It's just that I wasn't sure what to give you.*
GABRIEL: *No.*

These are the first lines of dialogue I wrote for *When the Rain Stops Falling*. They were written for a scene in an early workshop and remained in the final play. The scene takes place between a mother and her adult son. The fact that she is not sure what to give him for lunch reveals something about their relationship. Some kind of emotional distance exists between them. But I didn't know its cause.

What is eventually revealed, an act of betrayal in the past, is so central to the play that it is hard to believe that it was not the starting point. But it wasn't. The idea of emotional distance emerged in this snatch of dialogue. I then asked myself why. What caused it? Writing is the process by which you ask yourself a series of questions. In answering one question, another is posed. And so on. I look at those four lines now, almost written blind, and I can see the whole play in them.

5. Finding My Voice

I graduated from the VCA with a swirl of influences fighting for space in my head. Although the Australian Performing Group and the Pram Factory were no longer, their legacy remained. Most people who were working at that time, at least at La Mama and other independent venues, had come out of the APG or been a part of the rebirth of Australian theatre in the 1970s—the New Wave, as it was termed. The battles that this generation fought, to see our own stories and to hear our own language on stage, built the platform on which the writers of my generation stood. I didn't fully understand this at the time and found myself turning away from the robust naturalism and self-conscious nationalism of some of this work, seeking international influences instead.

I gravitated toward Jean Pierre Mignon's Australian Nouveau Theatre (Anthill). His productions of Molière and other classics didn't interest me. I found them mannered and culturally distant, although, they were what everyone was talking about at the time. Instead, I was inspired by the minimalism of Beckett's shorter plays—*Not I, Breath, Come and Go*. I'd been intrigued by Richard Murphet's *Slow Love*, again a play almost without spoken language; and I was thrown off balance by Nicholas Mosely's *Catastrophe Practice* and Eugene Ionesco's *The*

Killing Game. I was staying up late with friends talking about Chaos Theory and reading *The Dancing Wu Lai Masters* and John Berger's *Ways of Seeing.*

While I was at college I had begun to play with narrative fragmentation, simultaneous dialogue and point of view. I pursued these techniques through short works: *Like Whiskey on the Breath of a Drunk You Love* (Anthill, Five Dollar Theatre Company, 1992), *Distant Lights From Dark Places* (Chameleon Theatre at La Mama, 1994) and the Jane and Paula monologues in Deidre Rubenstein's *Confidentially Yours* (Playbox, 1998). The combination of the two earlier short works culminated in the play *Speaking in Tongues* (Griffin, 1996), which in turn became the film *Lantana* (2001). This is indicative of how I work. I find an idea and I keep working with it, in different forms and different contexts, exploring it from several angles and creating a body of interrelated works around a primary formal idea.

> *SONJA/JANE: So why are you here?*
> *PETE/LEON: I don't know.*
> *PETE: There's something inside saying/it's not enough*
> *LEON: It's not enough*
> *PETE: I'm a fool but/I want more*
> *LEON: I want more*
> *PETE: I just want more. I want to feel something.*
> *LEON: I just want to feel something.*
> *LEON/PETE: Something inside.*
> *LEON: Like when I was a kid.*
> *PETE: Something intense.*
> *LEON: Something that will make me stop.*

PETE: Something wrong./ I just want to feel something.
LEON: I just want to feel something.
PETE/LEON: Because I'm numb.

Leon, Pete, Sonja and Jane, *Speaking in Tongues1* (1996)

In the opening scene of *Speaking in Tongues,* two couples are engaging in one-night stands in different motel rooms. Their action and language are almost identical and each scene mirrors, echoes and replicates the other. The difference is that one couple goes through with the affair, and the other doesn't. In the following scene, the same technique of simultaneously spoken language and action is continued as each character returns to their spouse. The reveal is that each partner in the two respective marriages is illicitly involved with the partners of the other marriage. A quartet of betrayal. The play takes a familiar trope of an affair and by superimposing the scenes on one another somehow magnifies its themes of human folly and frailty. I've seen it played as a farce and as a serious emotional study. Strangely, both approaches seem to hold true.

The play breaks a number of conventions. It's written for an ensemble of four actors: two women and two men. In the second part, four new characters are introduced, played by the same actors; and the same themes of trust and betrayal are explored in a different set of relationships. Unlike most plays, it's not the characters that continue through the drama but the ideas and themes. The tone, comic in part one, becomes darker and more complex in part two; and the language becomes, in parts, even more fragmented as the emotional stakes are raised. There are narrative links between the two parts. Moments that are witnessed and described in part one are then played out in part two. A stranger described in part one becomes a featured character in part two. Something seen from a distance in part one is seen from close up in part two. The play is exploring perspective, showing how the meaning of an event changes depending on the angle from which it is being viewed.

An early influence here was the seminal British television series, *Talking to a Stranger*, written by John Hopkins. Later structural influences came from filmmakers such as Robert Altman *(Nashville, Shortcuts)*, Quentin Tarantino *(Pulp Fiction)*, and later still, Paul Thomas Anderson *(Magnolia)*. But it was Akira Kurosawa's *Rashomon* that first awakened me to the possibilities of this approach. The element common to them all is the simple idea that truth is subjective and that story is the sum of a number of characters' experiences rather than the experience or journey of a single protagonist. This is a common element in my work. I'm interested in how a set of events impacts upon a group, rather than simply an individual. The synthesis of all these influences and experimentation was the film, *Lantana,* which broke new ground in the Australian cinema.

We had become used to seeing ourselves represented through the exaggerated lens of the decade's most successful films, *Strictly Ballroom* (1992), *Muriel's Wedding* and *Priscilla, Queen of the Desert* (1994) and *The Castle* (1998). They were bright, comic, celebratory and outrageous depictions of our suburban heritage. And then a counterweight landed in the form of an atmospheric and serious relationship drama, shot in natural light, depicting an urban and emotionally articulate set of characters who navigate their way through the more serious issues of their lives. Importantly, the film bravely—or naively—crossed genres. It was both a relationship drama and a thriller. In my mind it had always been a study of relationships, masculinity and even class. But one of the crucial decisions I made was to open the film on the image of a woman's body, trapped in a tangle of overgrown lantana vine. Who is the woman? And who is responsible for her being there? This is the familiar language of the crime thriller and the decision opened the film up to a broader audience. I often wonder whether, had I left that scene in its chronological place, near the end of the film, would the film have been as successful?

I don't want to lose you… I couldn't bear it

Leon Zat, *Lantana* (2001)

6. 'Unionists, Sharpen Your Knives'

I had my first professional work produced in 1986, whilst I was still at officially at college. Roland Manderson, with whom I had studied at the VCA asked me to join the Ensemble Theatre Project in Canberra, to create a work about living in the national capital. The result was *An Ocean out My Window*. The title was ironic, given that Canberra was the only Australian capital without an ocean outside its window. This project used the principles that we had practised at VCA—of building a work through improvisation and collaboration to support the writing process. The play was well received by its audience and critics; and my first royalty cheque at the end was a significant symbolic moment.

This collaborative approach to creating work was consolidated and developed further when I joined the Melbourne Workers Theatre (MWT) in 1987. As its name suggests it was a left-wing theatre collective, supported by the Trade Union movement and dedicated to telling the stories of the working class and to representing a diversity of Australian voices. Steve Payne, Michael White and Patricia Cornelius formed the company under the banner of the Australia Council's Art and Working Life Program.

The funding was for a twelve-week project. It was never meant to last. But in time it developed a substantial body of work, and survived till 2012. It is one of the great stories of the Australian theatre.

The composer Irine Vela joined the company in 1987 at the same time I did. With Patricia she became one of the key long-term and influential artists associated with the MWT's work. For this initial project we were also joined by John Romeril as dramaturg and Russell Walsh as director. We were based on site at the Jolimont train maintenance yard on the edge of Melbourne's CBD.

The working conditions of the yard were being eroded. A skilled workforce that had once taken pride in maintaining the city's trains was becoming increasingly demoralised in the face of new technologies and increasing redundancies. This situation was being experienced all over the country due to the rise of economic rationalism, and we were there on site at Jolimont to document it.

We had twelve weeks to research, develop, write and rehearse the show. I wrote it largely at night, in a small (and freezing) Atco, beside the railway tracks. I worked through the night to ensure the performers had material for the following day. We called the emerging play *State of Defence,* an apt description of the mood in working class and union politics at the time.

Music was always integral to the company's work. The title of this chapter, 'Unionists, Sharpen Your Knives', was a line from one of Irine's songs. It referred to the Gordian knot, the central image of the play, and urged union members to take direct action and slice through their intractable problem. A strike is called, lives and relationships are placed under pressure and the workers are eventually defeated. It's a familiar but noble story in the working class tradition of dignity being found in defeat.

The work needed to be flexible in structure and form. It was to be performed at various worksites, in lunchrooms and on the back of trucks on building sites. It must be capable of being performed within the confines of a lunch break, and then expanded into a full-length work for an evening performance. This needed a dexterous approach to the writing. John was a steady and enthusiastic guide, drawing on his experience from the APG days, while the whole ensemble participated in the rigorous investigation needed for the process of creating the play. Everybody had the right to speak, to express an opinion and to offer an idea. It was a brilliant school in which to learn my craft. Crucial was learning how to hold an audience in difficult performance circumstances. If you can capture an audience from the back of a truck while cement is being poured nearby and steel rafters are being swung overhead, something is working. Performing this play for a workforce that was living through the very experience it depicted remains one of the most formative experiences of my career.

Working with MWT taught me how people's lives could be validated and enriched by having their own stories reflected back to them. I came to understand my task as a playwright as being less about telling my story or reflecting my experience and more about empowering those without a voice by telling their stories. I saw myself as developing a set of skills that could be made available to any group that needed to tell their story. Today arguments around privilege and the question of who has access and who gets to tell what story now complicate those earlier noble ambitions. However, it is not a principle I'm yet ready to abandon.

Patricia wrote the company's second play *Dusting Our Knees,* based on the 1986 Victorian nurses' strike. And I returned in 1988 to write *The Ballad of Lois Ryan,* which was based on the true story of a woman who was killed in an industrial accident at a Melbourne textile factory. She was dragged into the machine on which she was working.

The disability activist Lesley Hall had joined the company as its administrator late in 1987. It was a long walk from the front gate to our offices and rehearsal space on the other side of the Jolimont site. It was still an all-male workforce in the yard, and the women who worked with the company, Patricia, Irine and actors Kate Gillick and Laura Lattuada, had to fend off sexist comments as they made their way to work. Lesley had a severe curvature of the spine and walked with a stick. Her disability was very visible. As she made the walk between the gate and office she received derogatory comments about her appearance from some of the men. An arrangement could have been made to drive her across the site each day but Lesley insisted on walking. It was her intention to remain visible. Sometimes she would engage someone who was directing abuse towards her. He never did it again. Her strength of character and natural dignity won the respect of the Jolimont workforce. Every step she took on that long walk was a political act because it confronted ignorant men with their prejudice and changed the way people saw disability.

I tell this story because people like Lesley Hall are

often left out when the history is written. She epitomised a political spirit that informed what we did. As well as working the numbers, writing the grants and ensuring the company's future, she was a moral and intellectual force that helped shape and direct the company's work. The history of Melbourne Workers Theatre has been told in more detail elsewhere; but this early period was led by a committed group of powerful personalities. Sometimes we clashed and argued but we never lost sight of a shared purpose.

> *Hey, Jimmy, I need a job. Any jobs there?*
> *I can sell, I can sell, sure I can sell.*
> *I can sell anything.*
> *Ask you boss, go on, ask him for me.*
> *Tell him you've got a mate,*
> *Tell him I can sell. Tell him that.*

Martin, *State of Defence* (1987)

7. 1988

Some years are more significant than others. In 1988, I was 25 years old and Eugenia Fragos and I shocked our friends by getting married. We'd been living together since our first year of college in 1984 so it wasn't a big surprise to us. But in the world of the theatre, where sexual identity was fluid, and where so many had found refuge after rejecting the constraints and conventions of their upbringing, marriage, in a traditional sense, was rightly regarded with suspicion. For Eugenia, it was a return to her Greek-Australian culture. We were married in a Greek Orthodox Church; and afterwards we danced among the vines of her parents' vineyard, drank her father's home-made wine and ate a feast cooked by her mother and aunties. Within a few years we were making babies. We were in this respect simultaneously very old-fashioned and ahead of our time.

Earlier that year, our friend and colleague, the inspirational theatre director Ewa Czajor had been murdered in Thailand. She was on her way to study theatre in Warsaw and had stopped off for a brief holiday with her friend, the actor Peter Murphy. In that moment our youth came to an end. The first death among us was brutal and savage. The world was no longer innocent. Ewa left a gaping hole in the lives of many. Like so many of our theatre colleagues and friends, Eugenia and I were bereft. Eugenia had just worked with her in Joanna Murray-Smith's first play, *Angry Young Penguins*. Ewa was the hub of an interconnected network of theatre-makers in Melbourne in the 1980s. Had she lived and returned from her studies in Poland, as was her intention, she would have been one of the leaders of our profession.

At the time of her death I was working with the Melbourne theatre ensemble Whistling in the Theatre. They were a mix of graduates from the University of Melbourne and the VCA, including Tom Gutteridge, Polly Croke, Humphrey Bower, Bob Pavlich and Margaret Mills. Many of them were close to Ewa, having worked with her at Melbourne University's Union House Theatre.

Whistling in the Theatre was an ensemble made up of erudite thinkers and wonderful theatre makers who drew inspiration from their study of the classics and contemporary philosophy. They were the smart kids I never got to hang out with at school. In this new work they presented me with a brilliant premise. The idea was to draw a parallel between the medieval myth of the *Ship of Fools* and the recently introduced Work-For-the-Dole scheme. In his seminal work *Madness and Civilization*, Michel Foucault had used the Ship of Fools as an analogy for how governments treated outsiders—in this case the insane. We applied the same idea to the way our government planned to treat the unemployed. In medieval times, 'the fools' were placed on board a ship and sent off down the Rhine. In our play, the unemployed were put on a bus and sent into the desert on a work-for-the-dole scheme. In the course of the play these two groups become one in that place between time, which can only exist in the theatre.

On a night when all the good and all the sane
were safely sleeping in their beds, I lay awake
tormented by a storm raging outside my window.
As I reached out to close the shutters, a mighty
bolt of lightning struck, illuminating a wide vista
before me. I saw a vast sea, rough and churned by
a furious wind and a ship teetering on the crest of
a wave. A ship like none I had seen before—open
decked and laden with a fertile garden, with vines
for rigging bearing all manner of fruit. And where
the mast would normally stand there stood in its
place a tall and mighty birch. The ship's passengers
huddled together under the canopy of foliage,
some with their faces buried within their sodden
rags but others with theirs upturned to a black
heaven. And what at first I thought to be the ship's
figurehead, was in fact the figure of an old and
bent woman, her wild hair streaming behind her.
She seemed to be shouting something in the face
of the wind, either in great torrents of laughter
or hideous and horrific screams when suddenly
a large wave rose before her, sure to sweep her
into the sea. Then in an instant, light turned to
black and black back to light and old had become
young. Instead of the bent hag now stood a young
and proud woman, tall and strong with her arms
stretched before her. I could not tell if she was wel-
coming her imminent end or indeed fending it off
in a last defiant gesture against her fate.

The Fool, *Ship of Fools* (1988)

Ewa's death deepened a network of friendships in Melbourne. Peter Murphy, who was with her in Thailand, moved into the flat next door with our good friend, Tony Ayers. Peter spent days curled up in front of the heater in our flat, wearing Ewa's blue dressing gown. He was literally stricken with grief. It was a time when so many of my actor friends were out of work. It was as though Ewa's death had taken the wind out of our sails. Perhaps, theatre didn't mean much anymore.

What better way, then, to confront our grief than by doing a comedy?

After Dinner had originally been written in my first year at VCA as a short play for three female actors. Surprisingly, given what it became, it was a serious and moody work. I now sat down and rewrote it as black comedy, expanding it and introducing the two male figures. The primary aim was to create a part for Peter and for other friends who weren't working. Eugenia reprised the role of Paula that she had played at VCA. Kim Trengove, a fellow-student at VCA, played Dympie. Leigh Morgan, who had worked with Ewa and Eugenia on *Angry Young Penguins,* played the recently widowed Monika. Tom Gutteridge who had also been a member of the *Angry Young Penguins* cast played the hapless Gordon. And Peter took on the role of Stephen. We played a two-week season at La Mama, under the direction of Kim Durban, who had also been close friend of Ewa's. It was a hit. Not hard at La Mama with its capacity of fifty seats. But it had enough momentum to transfer to a six-week season at Theatre Works in St Kilda and then was picked up as a commercial work by

Hocking and Woods at the Universal Theatre in Fitzroy. This was unusual for a new Australian play. We were all a little shell-shocked by its success. Perhaps Ewa was watching over us.

I have seen people fall out of their chairs laughing at that play. As funny as it is, it is also a painful study of loneliness in the suburbs. If the balance between its comedy and its pathos can be found, then *After Dinner* can work beautifully.

> *But wait because there's more. Once I was on my back, Martin would straddle me, and from the fly of his pyjamas, his rubbed-raw, pointy red penis would be staring at me, dribbling his vile semen all over my nightie. Oh, yes, I tried to have children but I never could because Martin could rarely wait long enough to get inside me. That man. That lazy oaf of a man. I saw him lying in his own shit. And I refused to clean him up. I let his own mother come in and see him like that. I told her to clean up the shit.*
>
> Monika, *After Dinner* (1988)

As a rule in the theatre, if you think you have been too offensive or have gone too far, it is often worth going a little further.

1988 saw an eclectic range of work emerge. As well as *After Dinner* and *Ship of Fools,* I wrote *The Ballad of Lois Ryan* for Melbourne Workers Theatre and began working on

Holy Day, which had been commissioned by John Ellis, at the Church Theatre in Hawthorn. It was my capacity to work with very different groups, with different aesthetics, processes and approaches to theatre that enabled me to survive as a playwright in these early years of my career.

8. Who's Afraid?

In 1997, to mark the tenth anniversary of Melbourne Workers Theatre, the then Artistic Director, Susie Dee, invited a number of writers who had worked for the company to collaborate on a new play. This included playwright Melissa Reeves, Patricia Cornelius, Irine Vela and myself. We immediately made the decision to extend the invitation to a new voice so that the work marked not just the company's history but its future. Given Patricia's, Melissa's and my Anglo-Celtic heritage, we knew that this new voice must speak from a different place. I had just adapted Christos Tsiolkas's novel *Loaded,* for the film *Head On.* He was the perfect choice, vibrant, political and fiercely intelligent. The five of us came together for a two-week period of research and discussion and mapped out the play, which would become the seminal political work *Who's Afraid of the Working Class?*

The play was a savage critique of the Victorian Government led by Jeff Kennett. It depicted characters who had been left behind by the new economy and it warned that economic rationalism was in danger of creating an underclass that no longer identified with traditional working class values or institutions. It was a prescient work and caught the zeitgeist of the time. Directed by Julian Meyrick and performed at the Trade Union Town Hall in Carlton, it was a timely reminder just how powerful 'poor theatre' can be when the content has substance and relevance to its audience.

Who's Afraid of the Working Class? was unusual in that it grew out of the collaboration between five creators: four writers and a composer. Such projects too often flounder in conflicting opinion. But my memory of the conversations that took place around that table is that we were each genuinely excited by what the others had to say. It was as if our respective voices complemented and enhanced the others. Certainly, there was a synthesis of political views and the whole was greater than the sum of its parts; this showed in the work. For me it was a relief to share the responsibility. The weight of the play's meaning was carried equally by us all. The opening lines, penned by Christos and performed by a young actor, Bruce Morgan, went like this.

I love Jeff Kennett. I think he's a good guy, a sexy
guy. I like it that he's tall. I like it that he's smart.
I like it that he doesn't give a shit about anyone.
He's an arsehole, I know that. He's a cunt. It's
obvious. He's a silver-spoon-up-his-arse cunt...

There was a collective gasp in the audience. The State of Victoria had largely been cowed by Kennett's political muscle and he was about to have his cock pulled out of his pants and sucked off by some guy in a lift in Parliament house. It wasn't the first gasp that night. There were laughs and there were tears and there was deathly silence at unwatchable moments of pain.

I fell in love with my fellow writers in that project. I still love them. It's the conversation I crave. They make me a better writer. Eugenia is also an important part of this collaboration having performed in many of our respective works over the years, including *Who's Afraid of the Working Class?* We worked together again as a team, in *Fever* (2002), a play that creates a post-apocalyptic vision of a country riven by xenophobia. I don't think it was as successful as the earlier work. It lacked the unity of style and clarity of story. Patricia, on the other hand argues that *Fever* is a more ambitious and braver work than *Who's Afraid of the Working Class?* Certainly, we all extended ourselves as writers and pushed the collaboration beyond the limit it had reached in the earlier work.

This year Daniel Clarke from the Victorian Arts Centre has brought the five of us together again with a new commission to mark the twentieth anniversary of the original play. Like *Who's Afraid?* the brief is to consider the politics of the times. I won't pre-empt here where it might go but we begin as this paper goes to press with a two-week period of research and conversation. It will be interesting, in this time of identity politics and divisive public commentary, to see whether we can so boldly step across lines of class, race, gender, sexual orientation, and ethnicities. There was a kind of fearlessness to our previous work as we sought to speak from whatever position was required to support our argument. Now, it seems that there are more constraints around who can speak and on what. The conversation between us will be all the more interesting because of it. I feel confident, though, that we will find the way to say what needs to be said.

Carol says, 'Problem with you, Rhonda, problem with you is that you're just too fertile. You've just got to look at a man and you're up the duff.' And we laughed but she's right, she's fucking right. Woman from Welfare says, 'It must be hard. Must be hard for you Rhonda, with all those kids. Looking after them, it must be hard.' And I say, 'No, it's not hard.' But it is. I know it and she knows it too. But I'm not Going to give her the satisfaction. So I say, 'No. Those kids, those kids are my blessings. You understand? Everyone of them. A blessing.'

Rhonda, *Who's Afraid of the Working Class* (1998)

9. Becoming a Screenwriter

Most of my work in the theatre has come out of various collaborative processes. Writing for film has proved to be, by and large, a more solitary engagement.

The international premiere of *Lantana* took place at the Toronto Film Festival on 11 September 2001. That morning terrorists had flown two planes into the World Trade Centre in New York and the world changed. The audience, understandably, were somewhat distracted. Nevertheless, the film subsequently captured a significant audience in the USA and Europe; suddenly another metaphorical fish fell at my feet and I found myself in demand as an international screenwriter. How quickly, that door opened that had always seemed shut tight. I stepped through it having little idea what I would find.

My career as a screenwriter had begun in 1990 when Baz Luhrmann invited me to work with him on *Strictly Ballroom*. This turned out to be a steep learning curve in the craft of screenwriting. The lesson was not to over-complicate things. Baz and Catherine Martin, his creative partner, had a clear and original vision, which was so evident in the eventual film. Fresh from the school of MWT, I attempted to locate the story in the working class politics of a Wollongong steel mill—the nominal setting of the film. It proved to be a distraction from a simple and charming plot. Baz was encouraging as I wrestled with the screenplay but it eventually became clear that he needed to move in another direction. He went on to work with Craig Pearce, who had a better understanding of what was required and became Baz's longstanding collaborator. The film's success is now legendary but it was not one in which I shared. I left the film grateful for the experience and full of respect for what they achieved.

In 1991 I was awarded a Literature Board attachment to the Australian Film, TV and Radio school, in Sydney. Here I had access to the school's extensive film library. The work of John Cassavetes was particularly influential: *A Woman under the Influence, Shadows, Opening Night, Faces.* Whilst Cassavetes' work is undeniably cinematic, it is the human figure in crisis that remains the focus. I also discovered Robert Altman's *Nashville,* which opened up the possibility of alternative story structures as well as many other masterpieces of the cinema.

A series of television plays followed in the early 1990s. *Piccolo Mondo* (SBS, 1991), *Lust* in the *Seven Deadly Sins* series (ABC, 1994) and perhaps the most successful of them, the semi-autobiographical *The Fisherman's Wake,* from the *Naked* series (ABC, 1996), directed by Neil Armfield. This began my fortunate collaboration with the producer, Jan Chapman. All three TV plays were contained within their dramatic situation: a lunch between three female friends, a dinner party that goes wrong, the gathering of a family after the death of a father. They could just as easily have been works for the theatre. I hadn't yet begun to think and write cinematically.

Jan commissioned me to adapt Tim Winton's novel *The*

Riders for the director, Ray Lawrence. When Fred Scully's wife Jennifer fails to show up at the airport in Dublin, he begins a tense odyssey through Europe in search of her, dragging their daughter Billie with him. He never finds Jennifer or discovers the reason why she left him. Instead, he comes face to face with his limitations as a husband and father, and as a man. Perhaps the answer to the mystery lies there. To research the film I followed Scully's footsteps through Ireland, Greece, Paris and Amsterdam. The material demanded that I come to terms with a more visual way of storytelling. I had to learn to write in images.

We worked on the project for three years but in the end we were unable to make the film. It was difficult to raise the finance and the rights were sold to another party. This was a bitter lesson to learn: that just because you write a film, it doesn't mean that it will be made.

Jan Chapman and Ray Lawrence were at the opening night of *Speaking in Tongues* at the Griffin in Sydney in 1996. Still nursing our wounds from having lost *The Riders,* we discussed the possibility of basing a film on this play. I had previously written a treatment based on a version of the story, so I already had the film in my head. I could see it. But it took a lot more work to get it onto the page. Adapting my own work was challenging but I felt a certain freedom to reinvent the material as required. There was no author looking over my shoulder.

Writing a screenplay is similar to writing a poem. The aim is to express as much meaning as possible by using as few words as possible. It is a distilled form of storytelling, which is achieved through writing a series of drafts, which hone and refine the material. Like a poem, there is a form and a set of rules to which one usually adheres. Take for, example, a sonnet. It consists of 14 lines. The first 12 include three quatrains of four lines each. Each quatrain establishes a theme or problem, which is then resolved in the final couplet. There is something exquisite in the formality of this pattern. The rules of writing a screenplay aren't quite so rigid, and yet if you understand them and are comfortable to work within them, they can be liberating. Creating a story, in film or theatre, is about making a series of choices. Those choices are easier to make if you are working within a pre-determined frame.

The place of the writer in the process of filmmaking is very different from their place in the theatre. In theatre the playwright is central to realising the vision, if it is based on a written text, and particularly in the case of a new play. In this case, the writer belongs in the rehearsal room and I have never worked with a director who didn't want me to be there. The task is to be a strong and curious, presence whilst ensuring that you give the director and cast the room to discover the play. I go into a rehearsal room ready to discover it with them, and not as the one who already knows the answers.

The relationship between the screenwriter and the film is different, according to whether it is an original story or an adaptation. In the case of the former, I would expect to remain with the film through its shooting and its editing process. This was the case in *Lantana*. Ray, Jan and I remained in close conversation throughout making the film and crucially in the editing process, where significant shifts to the structure of the story were made. For example, in the script the disappearance of Valerie Summers took place toward the end of the second act. It is, in fact the moment that turns us toward the crisis and climax of the film. In the editing process we observed that the film was lacking energy and drive through some of the second act. Our solution was to move Valerie's disappearance forward, which raised the dramatic stakes earlier and gave the rest of the act greater momentum. This was only possible because Ray, the director, was confident enough in his own vision to invite me into his process, just as I had invited him into the writing process. Let me be clear: just as it was important that Ray allowed me a degree of autonomy to write the screenplay, it was essential that I allowed him the room to find the film through the editing process. I was not in the edit room every day. I watched the evolving cut once a week and responded accordingly.

Not all my experiences working on Australian films have been so successful and rewarding. Other directors have not been so welcoming; and the filmmaking process itself has excluded me as soon as my job was perceived to be completed. This has been the experience of many screenwriters. They find themselves left behind by a process in which until then they have been intimately embedded. The joke is that the only person without a job on the film set is the screenwriter. We end up feeling redundant because essentially our job is done. In the case of an adaptation, I accept this. But if the work is my own, either an original story or based on a play I have written, then I cannot accept those terms. That's not the way I want to work. In the end it's about the quality of our relationships; the mutual respect that is held among the film's key creative personnel. If the respect and trust between the director and the screenwriter breaks down, invariably the film will not meet its expectations.

In the case of an international adaptation, the distance between the screenwriter and the final result is usually greater. Often, I am not around when the film is being made. I am working on a different project by then. Film remains primarily a director's medium and the film will ultimately represent his or her vision. This is not to undervalue the role of the screenwriter. On the contrary, I see my role as one of the team of skilled creators and technicians required to make the film, similar to the editor and the cinematographer. Each has their role to play in a highly calibrated process and the end result reflects everybody's contribution.

Most of the international films I have worked on are adaptations of other writers' novels. So it is not a question of bringing my own voice to bear on the work but channelling that of the author. It always remains their story. My task is to tell it in a different medium from the one for which it was originally created. The challenge in adaptation is to create for the audience a similar emotional experience to the one they would have by reading the book. To do so, some adaptations require significant changes in plot, simply because there is less time for the story to unfold and less access to the interior world of the characters. Story must be largely conveyed through what is said and done, rather than by description of interior thoughts and motives. The important thing is to maintain the tone and feel of the book.

I am currently working on the adaptation of the novel *Stoner* by American writer John Williams. Published in 1965, it tells the story of William Stoner, the son of impoverished mid-western farmers, from 1910 to his death as a respected academic in the late 1950s. It is the story of a life and a young man's discovery of language. It is a beautifully spare novel. Not much actually happens in terms of plot and yet so much happens. In adapting the book I have sought to maintain the novelist's style, creating visual moments of silence and stillness in which the camera can linger upon the character's face and body in the mid-western landscape. This is the kind of film where meaning relies not so much on what is said but on what is not said. Often, the dialogue is used to frame the moment. It is in the moments between speaking that the interior world of the character can be revealed.

Following the success of *Lantana*, I accepted a number of offers to work on high-profile adaptations. I was flattered. I was excited. I was terrified. I took on too many projects and spread myself too thinly across a difficult slate of work. It was stressful keeping several projects in the air and meeting the demands of American and British producers whilst working from Australia. I worked like this for a number of years. I wrote myself into a premature middle age. Most of those projects weren't made and the one that was, *Edge of Darkness,* based on the seminal 1980s BBC TV series written by Troy Kennedy Martin and starring Mel Gibson, was taken away from me at the very end. As can happen in Hollywood. As a result of these stalled projects I lost some of what should have been the most productive years of my writing life and found myself in the midst of a debilitating bout of writer's block. Another word for it is depression. I had been distracted from my own journey as a writer and had lost some of my confidence and spirit. I had no one to blame but myself.

It is difficult as a freelance screenwriter, still building a career, not to accept offers of work when they come. There is the very real need to earn a living in what is a precarious profession. The fact is that I saw good reason to undertake every project I accepted. They were interesting books, often with talented directors and experienced producers attached, and they allowed me to work in the American and European film industries. Screenplays are incredibly difficult documents to get right. They need to be both a practical and artistic document, serving the purpose of an architectural blueprint, a selling document and a point of inspiration to all who will come to work on it. Whether a film is made or not lies largely beyond the screenwriter's control, no matter how well written the screenplay might be.

Many writers can testify to how terrifying and debilitating writer's block can be. I have learned to accept it as an inevitable part of the process. It is a forced time to reflect on my approach to my work. And in the end there is only one solution—to keep writing.

10. Finding My Way Back

I'm older now and more discerning. I'm not so easily flattered and I say 'No' more often than not. I take on the projects that count and I no longer fear that the phone will stop ringing. I'll be ok if it does. Most importantly, I maintain a balance between writing for film and theatre and I'm finding a happy medium between the two in writing for television. Its recent renaissance is writer-driven and it's a medium with a voracious appetite for good stories.

I rediscovered my confidence as a screenwriter adapting the John Le Carré novel, *A Most Wanted Man* (2014). Typical of Le Carré's work, it has a complicated and labyrinthine plot. So much of adapting a book is about deciding what to keep and what to lose. Screenwriting is about the management of information. Knowing what to withhold from the audience and what to reveal and when. I found myself, in this case, working with an instinctual understanding of where the emphasis needed to be placed, whilst also successfully retaining the distinctive Le Carré feel. The film was directed by Anton Corbijn, the Dutch photographer, and starred the wonderful actor Philip Seymour Hoffman. Tragically, it was to be his last film. He died shortly after its premiere at the Sundance Film Festival.

I rediscovered my spirit as a writer by turning back to the theatre and writing *When the Rain Stops Falling*. The director, Chris Drummond, had created the circumstances in which a conversation could unfold over a number of years, between several artists who shared a growing concern about climate change, including the visual artist, Hossein Valamanesh. We took some rough ideas into a workshop with a group of generous actors and began to create the world of the play. It reminded me of what I love about the theatre, the conversation and collaboration and the sense of connection.

The play was beautifully realised in its first production at the 2008 Adelaide Festival of the Arts and it toured to most capital cities over the next few years. It went on to be produced in separate productions in London at the Almeida and in New York at the Lincoln Centre and has now been produced in many different languages, including Spanish in the acclaimed 2015/16 production *Cuando deje de Llover*, directed by Julian Fuentes.

Meanwhile, *The Secret River* afforded me the opportunity to work on an epic scale and about a subject of consequence to our national identity. I was fortunate to work with some of the best exponents of the theatre in the country: Neil Armfield, Stephen Page, Stephen Curtis, Tess Schofield, Mark Howett and Iain Grandage. And Kate Grenville's book demanded the best of us.

The project was initiated by Cate Blanchett and Andrew Upton, as artistic directors of the Sydney Theatre Company. They invited Neil Armfield and Stephen Page to work together. I joined the conversation soon after and the three of us wrestled with finding a conceptual approach to the work. As we were each working in different countries and on other projects at the time, it was difficult to get us in the room together. I was based in New York and working on *A Most Wanted Man*. We also felt the weight of responsibility to get it right, given the sensitivities of the material. At times we felt quite despondent and overwhelmed by the task but three days spent at Neil's house on the Hawkesbury River allowed us to imagine the play in the place it was set.

Eventually, a number of decisions allowed us to break through the uncertainty. We decided to cut the English section of the novel. Ironically, it felt as though we were more familiar with Dickensian London than we were with our own historical narratives. Losing this section allowed us to focus on the central narrative moment in the play—the meeting of black and white over disputed land.

The biggest decision we made was to give the Dharug characters language. In the book the Indigenous people are seen through the eyes of the white settlers. They are held at a distance. In the play they needed to have a more active presence in the story. They needed what all characters on stage need—motivation, attitude, emotion and an interior life. Dharug elder and songman, Richard Green, joined the process and crucially gave the characters names and language in the scenes I had created.

Furthermore, we decided to embody the river as witness and narrator of the story. She became known as Dhirrumbin, the Dhurag name for the river. It was her role to relate the tragic tale. This difficult and emotional task was undertaken by two of our great stage actors, Ursula

Yovich in the 2013 season and Ningali Lawford-Wolf in the 2016 and 2017 remounts.

Finally, we decided that this story at its simplest was about two families who lived on different sides of the same point. They had different cultures and histories and very different relationships to, and understanding of, the land on which they lived, and this would eventually bring them into terrible conflict. The rightful owners of the land were never in doubt but, as families, they shared much in common, and this commonality hinted at the possibility of a very different history. This missed opportunity lay at the heart of the play's tragedy.

We took these ideas and starting points into a workshop with actors and the design team. Design ideas from Stephen Curtis and Tess Schofield began to emerge and influence the writing process, as did the composer Iain Grandage's method of working with cast members on the floor. Neil's direction was the point at which all these influences began to synthesise. He had worked with many of the creative team before and they already had a shared language and understanding of how the process would evolve. It was in the workshop that we collectively discovered the theatrical language of the production.

With this understanding, I wrote the play over an intense three-month period, sending Stephen and Neil sections of work as I completed them. With the script complete we gathered again for a second workshop. Minimal changes were made to the text, except for the ending. It was difficult to get the nuance right and we tried many endings before settling on the final moments in production week.

In the end the production reached a broad audience across the country and it has set something of a benchmark, reminding us of how important it is to tell the stories of national significance on our big stages. To do so we need our theatre companies and their supporters to invest in long-term development. Both *When the Rain Stops Falling* and *The Secret River* were marinated over a long period of time and supported with workshop development.

Following *The Secret River,* I turned back to a more intimate and domestic work. *Things I Know to be True* evokes the suburban world in which I grew up. It is a loving, nostalgic and in the end tragic, portrait of a family in crisis. It unfolds through the four seasons of a year as the parents, Bob and Fran, weather the crises of identity in their four adult children's lives.

> *We spoilt you… You and your sister. We brought you up to think that you can have what you want, you can be what you want. No matter what the cost. Or who it hurts. People like us. Your father and me. The mugs we are. We're just the people we were told to be. And who was I told to be? A mother. Well, I wish I'd never had children.*
>
> Fran, *Things I Know to Be True* (2016)

This play was co-produced by the State Theatre Company of South Australia and UK-based Frantic Assembly. It was co-directed by Geordie Brookman and Scott Graham. As has become customary to my work, we built the world of the play through a workshop process, creating characters and dramatic situations by improvisation before I even began to write. Frantic Assembly creates a distinctive physical language in their work. I was mindful of this as I wrote the play, understanding that monologues provided more scope than dialogue-driven scenes for the physical movement and image making that the directors sought to explore. Hence, there is a series of monologues built into the structure. Again, the point is that, as a playwright, I needed to respond to the aesthetics of the companies for which I was creating the work .

The play opened in Adelaide in May 2016 with an Australian cast. The same production then opened in London, in September, at the Lyric Hammersmith, with a British cast. It returns to London later this year before beginning a UK tour.

> *Once I saw her, Mum, bawling her eyes out and banging her head against the trunk of that tree. I was twelve. I had never seen her cry. Not once. Not even when her own mother died. And everything I thought was certain about the world changed. I went back inside and turned the television on. I was scared. What makes a woman cry like that? A mother. My mother. I didn't understand and I didn't have the courage to ask her. Now, that I am a woman, married with children of my own I don't need to, I know exactly why a woman bashes her head against the trunk of a tree.*
>
> Pip, *Things I Know to Be True*

11. State of Play

I began this paper by making a distinction between the work of the playwright and the work of other writers, such as novelists and poets. I wanted to draw attention to the collaborative nature of the playwright's role. Unlike other writers who work in isolation, we belong to a broad fraternity of mutually dependent theatre makers: actors, directors, designers and composers. Great theatre comes out of the relationship between these disciplines and our theatre companies are able to bring them together under the same roof.

Recent initiatives from two of our major companies recognise the need for playwrights to be a part of a company's culture and fabric. Earlier this year the Sydney Theatre Company announced an Emerging Writers Group. Four young writers have been selected to work with the company's artists and literary manager over the course of a year. They will attend rehearsals and productions and they will also work with the company's Patrick White Fellow.

This fellowship is for an established writer. It includes a writer-in-residence position and a new commission. Previous fellows have included Raimondo Cortese, Patricia Cornelius, Hilary Bell, Angela Betzien, Kate Mulvany and Tommy Murphy. Each year, the Fellowship takes on its own form, according to the interests of the Fellow. I have received the Fellowship in 2017. As a part of my residency, I will work with the STC's emerging writers group. Mentorship is an important part of what needs to take place to ready young writers for a professional career.

Melbourne Theatre Company in their recently announced Next Wave initiative has included a $4.6 million dollar investment in writer development. It offers 35 new commissions and 15 writer-in-residence positions over the next three years.

Commissions, however, are worthless unless they lead to production. Development is not an end in itself. The argument needs to be made that the companies should only commission where there is the real intent to produce. And if the development process isn't leading to a play that can be programmed, then there is something lacking in the process; or the reason for the commission was unclear in the first place. Scattering money in untargeted commissions across a large number of playwrights has proved unsuccessful in the past and deeply frustrating to the writers.

The Next Wave initiative indicates a move away from this approach. In embedding writers into the life and work of the company, through residencies, the MTC emulates the model practised by some of the most successful producers of new work, such as the Royal Court and National Theatre in London and the Public and Signature Theaters in New York.

Expectations will be high but these initiatives and others suggest a genuine commitment from our major companies to writer development. They want great

Australian plays. And more importantly, so do their audiences. Australian audiences are not satisfied with a repertoire only of Noel Coward, Anton Chekhov, Henrik Ibsen and William Shakespeare. They want new plays that tell their stories and reflect their lives. Box office results continue to prove that audiences favour contemporary work over the classics. There will always be room for both but contemporary Australian writing and the Australian canon need to remain the central purpose of our theatre.

I feel optimistic about the state of our theatre. I'm impressed by the quality of the writing I'm seeing, and excited by the ambition in ideas and scale of the work being undertaken. I will continue to argue for a theatre that prioritises the work of Australian playwrights, in all their diversity. I know that through such writing it is possible to read the pulse of the nation. I want to see new work by our established writers and I want to see the work of new playwrights being introduced each year. I want to see plays produced in a range of styles, and more than once, so that their writers have the opportunity to develop and to find new audiences.

I know that it's vital to see the works of our Australian canon revisited and reimagined for each new generation and that new generations of directors and actors have the opportunities to explore their theatrical heritage. It's also important to see the best new writing from around the world produced on our stages. This is as important as seeing the best of our own work on the stages of Europe, America and Asia. Australian playwrights should understand that their potential audience extends beyond Australia's national borders. Travel. See work. Make connections.

Some writers burn quickly and brightly and produce an extraordinary body of work in a short time. Others attain early success and then simply repeat themselves. I want every piece I write to be different from those that preceded it. Although, there will always be common themes and approaches to process, I want to venture into new ground each time I write a play. I'm in it for the long haul. I still believe my best work is ahead of me. I have to believe that. But, in order to ensure that's the case, I need to keep learning.

In December I begin a collaboration in Madrid, with the Spanish director of *When the Rain Stops Falling (Caundo deje de Llover),* Julian Fuentes. We will be resident at the multi-performance space, the Matadero, which is funding a six-month development project. We will work with various other artists from several disciplines over the course of the six months, including some of the actors who worked on *Caundo deje de Llover.* I will travel to Spain several times to undertake the work. Our investigation is open-ended and will explore the form of theatre in the twenty-first century as much as it will investigate ideas of content and story. It will eventually lead to a new work or series of works in various disciplines.

In any other industry, this work would be regarded as vital research and development. In Europe they are perhaps more aware of the value of such work and are more prepared to invest in the development of their artists. It's essential that in Australia, we make the argument for the importance of such explorative processes; for it's through such work that we will continue to expand and renew the art form.

I look forward to returning from Spain and using my experience there as a model to continue my own practice here. As a playwright I want a meaningful relationship with the people and companies that produce my work. I don't just want to be a visitor. I want to belong. I want to collaborate. I want to make theatre with other people who share a passion for it.

> *Forgive me... You let people go, Son. I have let people go all my life. I have run away from love. I don't know what all these things mean. It's not much. It's hardly anything at all. I can only tell you that somewhere at the end of this mess is where you belong... And now it's time to eat that fish.*
>
> Gabriel York, *When the Rain Stops Falling*

That's it. That's the nature of the fish. I hope it's a little clearer now.

Bibliography

Published Works:

After Dinner. Sydney: Currency Press, 1989.

The Ballad of Lois Ryan. Melbourne: *Australian Drama Studies*, La Trobe University, 1990.

Strictly Ballroom (with Baz Luhrmann and Craig Pearce). Sydney: Currency Press, 1993.

Scenes from a Separation (with Hannie Rayson). Sydney: Currency Press, 1996.

Confidentially Yours (devised and edited by Deirdre Rubinstein) Jane and Paula monologues. Sydney: Currency Press, 1998.

Speaking in Tongues. Sydney: Currency Press, 1998; New York: Dramatists Play Service, 2003; London, Nick Hern Books, 2009.

Holy Day. Sydney: Currency Press, 2001.

Lantana, Sydney: Currency Press, 2001.

When the Rain Stops Falling. Sydney: Currency Press, 2009; London: Nick Hern Books, 2009; New York: Dramatist Play Service, 2011.

The Secret River. Sydney: Currency Press, 2013.

Who's Afraid of the Working Class. Sydney: Currency Press, 2014.

Things I Know to be True. London: Nick Hern Books, 2016; Sydney: Currency Press, 2017.

Articles and Books

Amanda Duthie (editor), *Andrew Bovell: The Alchemy of Collaboration*, an anthology of reflections. Adelaide: Wakefield Press, 2015.

Melissa Reeves, *Pulling Rabbits Out of Hats,* a Response to *Speaking in Tongues.* Cue the Chorus series. Sydney: Currency Press, 2013.

Wesley Enoch: *Still Waters,* a Response to *The Secret River.* Cue the Chorus series. Sydney: Currency Press, 2014.

Speeches

Australian Writers Foundation and Foxtel Screenwriters' Address. Melbourne: The Wheeler Centre, October 2012.

https://www.wheelercentre.com/events/awf-foxtel-screenwriter-s-address-andrew-bovell

Playwriting Australia, National Play Festival, Keynote Address. Sydney, June 2014.

http://www.pwa.org.au/npf14-keynote-transcript/

BAFTA International Screenwriters' Address, London, Sept, 2015.

http://www.bafta.org/film/features/andrew-bovell-delivers-his-screenwriters-lecture

COPYRIGHT
INFORMATION

PLATFORM PAPERS
Quarterly essays from Currency House Inc.
Founding Editor: Dr John Golder
Editor: Katharine Brisbane
Currency House Inc. is a non-profit association and resource centre advocating the role of the performing arts in public life by research, debate and publication.

Postal address: PO Box 2270, Strawberry Hills, NSW 2012, Australia
Email: info@currencyhouse.org.au Tel: (02) 9319 4953
Website: www.currencyhouse.org.au Fax: (02) 9319 3649

Editorial Committee: Katharine Brisbane AM, Michael Campbell, Dr Robin Derricourt, Professor Julian Meyrick, Martin Portus, Dr Nick Shimmin, Greig Tillotson

ISBN 978-0-9946130-4-2
ISSN 1449-583X

Author's photograph by Jeremy Shaw Photography

Typeset in Garamond
Printed by McPherson's Printing Group

Production by XOU Creative

FORTHCOMING

PP No.53, November 2017

THEATRE FOR YOUNG AUDIENCES:
When will they let us play
with the big kids?

One of Australia's best-loved writers for young audiences in books, plays and TV programs, mourns the lack of attention to the process of making live entertainment for the young. Its creators are often more inventive with visual imagery, story structure. puppetry and electronic effects than text-based playwriting for adults; but it is secretly assumed that kids will be less critical of mediocre production than adults. He asks whether stage and film adaptations of popular children's books are a benefit or are making it harder for original scripts to get a hearing; and he looks to other ways of moving forward.

Richard Tulloch has written more than 60 children's books and adaptations for the stage. He first came to notice in the 1980s, writing for the TV characters Bananas in Pyjamas, for whom he has published many books. His work is equally admired in Europe where he and his family have a second home in Amsterdam.